LEADERS LIKE US

Jackie Ormes

Reader Choice Title

The subject of this Reader Choice title was chosen by readers and educators. We are proud to bring you titles, topics, and stories that reflect the choices and voices of our diverse and brilliant readers!

BY J. P. MILLER

ILLUSTRATED BY AMANDA QUARTEY

Rourke Educational Media

A Division of Carson Dellosa Education

BEFORE AND DURING READING ACTIVITIES

Before Reading: *Building Background Knowledge and Vocabulary*

Building background knowledge can help children process new information and build upon what they already know. Before reading a book, it is important to tap into what children already know about the topic. This will help them develop their vocabulary and increase their reading comprehension.

Questions and Activities to Build Background Knowledge:

1. Look at the front cover of the book and read the title. What do you think this book will be about?
2. What do you already know about this topic?
3. Take a book walk and skim the pages. Look at the table of contents, photographs, captions, and bold words. Did these text features give you any information or predictions about what you will read in this book?

Vocabulary: *Vocabulary Is Key to Reading Comprehension*

Use the following directions to prompt a conversation about each word.

- Read the vocabulary words.
- What comes to mind when you see each word?
- What do you think each word means?

Vocabulary Words:
- *arthritis*
- *caricatures*
- *diversity*
- *exaggerated*
- *independent*
- *proofreader*
- *sculptures*
- *syndicated*

During Reading: *Reading for Meaning and Understanding*

To achieve deep comprehension of a book, children are encouraged to use close reading strategies. During reading, it is important to have children stop and make connections. These connections result in deeper analysis and understanding of a book.

 Close Reading a Text

During reading, have children stop and talk about the following:

- Any confusing parts
- Any unknown words
- Text to text, text to self, text to world connections
- The main idea in each chapter or heading

Encourage children to use context clues to determine the meaning of any unknown words. These strategies will help children learn to analyze the text more thoroughly as they read.

When you are finished reading this book, turn to the next-to-last page for **Text-Dependent Questions** and an **Extension Activity**.

TABLE OF CONTENTS

THE NEW GIRL IN TOWN

Have you ever attended an event and you were different from everyone else there? Maybe you were the only person of your gender or race in the room. How did it make you feel? What things would you do to make everyone feel included? Jackie Ormes made sure that African Americans were included in comics. Her characters were bold, beautiful, and Black. She was a leader in **diversity**.

The character Torchy Brown danced her way out of Mississippi and into the bright city lights of Harlem, New York. She wanted to sing and dance at the Cotton Club. She wanted to be **independent**. Her fashion made people stop and stare. She was the new girl in town.

Torchy Brown was not real. Jackie had created Torchy and other characters for the *Dixie to Harlem* comic strip. It was one of the first American comic strips with an all-Black cast.

For young Jackie, soap was for more than bathing. She cut, shaped, and smoothed it to make soap **sculptures**. It was the start to her life as an artist.

By high school, Jackie knew she wanted to work in art. She drew cartoons and wrote for her school's yearbook. She was the yearbook's art director in high school.

BLACK EXCELLENCE

In Jackie's time, Black artists were not respected by many others in their industry. Black people were usually depicted as **caricatures**. Their lips, hair, and skin were **exaggerated**. The drawings were hurtful.

Jackie knew this wasn't fair or right. She wanted to show the whole world Black excellence: Black people being the best they could be without letting anything stop them. She could do this through her art.

RISE OF BLACK NEWSPAPERS
After World War II, there was an increase in Black-owned newspapers. They were very popular in big cities with large Black populations. Editors wrote about racism and unfair policies.

First, Jackie had to find a job. She wanted the freedom to create. She got a job with a newspaper called the *Pittsburgh Courier*. Jackie started out as a writer and **proofreader**. Later, she started creating comics. Leadership was just around the corner for her.

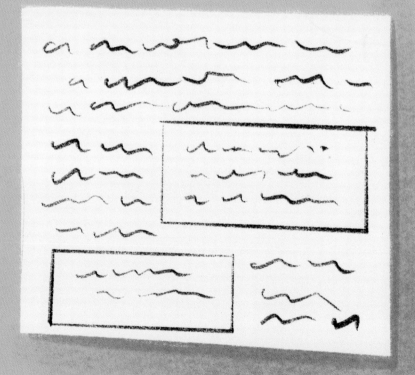

Jackie's career jumped off fast. In 1931, she married her sweetheart, Earl Ormes. The couple moved to Chicago in 1936. By 1937, she had created the *Dixie to Harlem* comic strip featuring Torchy Brown. A lot of people could relate to Torchy. Like Torchy, they had also left the American South for a better life up north. Jackie gave them hope.

Jackie's comics told Black stories differently than how they had been told before. She showed the characters she created having happy lives.
They **wore fashionable clothes...**
...had nice homes...
...and did exciting things.

A FASHION LEADER
Jackie was well-known among people who designed clothes. She learned how to influence people and make them want to buy certain clothes. She was in high demand as a fashion model.

ACTIVISM ON THE PAGE

Jackie began making her next comic strip, *Candy*. It was about a maid who worked in a big city. Candy was sweet and also said exactly what was on her mind. Jackie's third comic strip featured her character Torchy Brown. It was called *Torchy in Heartbeats*, and it showed Torchy's adventures as she tried to find love.

Torchy Brown in Heartbeats and *Candy* became popular. So did Jackie. She was the first Black woman in America to have nationally **syndicated** comic strips.

Jackie didn't stop creating. She made another comic strip, *Patty-Jo 'n' Ginger*. Jackie's character Ginger was a college graduate. Ginger's younger sister, Patty-Jo, never kept her opinions to herself. They said and did what most Black people in America weren't allowed to do or say. *Patty-Jo 'n' Ginger* was Jackie's longest-running comic strip.

Little Black girls loved Patty-Jo. The character was beautiful, smart, and looked like them. Jackie worked with a toymaker to create a Patty-Jo doll. The doll had beautiful clothes, brown skin, and silky hair. Patty-Jo was America's first Black character doll.

Jackie wanted every young Black girl to be able to have a beautiful doll, so she designed some made of paper. These paper dolls looked like Torchy Brown. They had gorgeous gowns, dresses, shoes, and hats. They were best sellers!

By 1956, Jackie had developed **arthritis** in her hands, and she retired. Jackie had been a role model for Black people for 20 years. The characters in her comics were inspirations for many people. She died in 1985. People didn't forget who Jackie was, though. In 2014, she was inducted into the National Association of Black Journalists Hall of Fame. In 2018, she was inducted into the Will Eisner Comic Industry Hall of Fame.

> **Jackie's philosophy of life was that you don't wait for someone to encourage you to do things. If you want to do it, then do it.**
> —Delores Towles, sister of Jackie Ormes

TIME LINE

1911   Jackie Ormes is born Zelda Mavin Jackson on August 11th to William and Mary Brown Jackson in Monongahela, Pennsylvania.

1929–30 Jackie works as the Art Director for the Monongahela High School yearbook.

1930   She graduates from Monongahela High School.

1931   Jackie marries accountant Earl Ormes and moves to Ohio. The couple has a daughter, who dies at three years old.

1936   Jackie starts working for the *Pittsburgh Courier* as a reporter and writer.

1937   On May 1st, Jackie's first comic strip, *Dixie to Harlem*, appears in the *Pittsburgh Courier*.

1942   Jackie moves to Chicago, Illinois.

1945   Her comic *Candy* runs from March 24th to July 25th.

1946   Her comic *Patty-Jo 'n' Ginger* begins running in the *Pittsburgh Courier*. The comic runs for 11 years.

1956   Jackie retires due to rheumatoid arthritis.

1985   She dies in Chicago on December 26th at the age of 74.

2014   Jackie is inducted into the National Association of Black Journalists Hall of Fame.

2018   Jackie is inducted into the Will Eisner Comic Industry Hall of Fame.

GLOSSARY

arthritis (ar-THRYE-tis): a disease in which joints become swollen and painful

caricatures (KAR-i-kuh-choors): exaggerated drawings or verbal descriptions of someone

diversity (di-VUR-si-tee): having a variety or many different kinds, especially kinds of people

exaggerated (ig-ZAJ-uh-rayted): made to seem bigger or more extreme than it really is

independent (in-di-PEN-duhnt): not controlled or affected by other people

proofreader (PROOF-reed-ur): someone who reads something carefully and corrects any mistakes in spelling, punctuation, and grammar that they find

sculptures (SKUHLP-churz): items carved or shaped out of stone, wood, marble, soap, or clay

syndicated (sin-dih-CAY-ted): published in many different newspapers in many places

INDEX

TEXT-DEPENDENT QUESTIONS

1. What was the title of Jackie Ormes' first comic strip?
2. Why was *Dixie to Harlem* important?
3. How did Jackie Ormes get started making art?
4. How was Jackie Ormes a leader in toys?
5. Why did Jackie Ormes retire from making comic strips?

EXTENSION ACTIVITY

Think about an issue that is important to you. What do you want people to know about this issue? Make your own comic strip or other piece of art about the issue.

ABOUT THE AUTHOR

J. P. Miller Growing up, J. P. Miller loved reading stories that she could become immersed in. As a writer, she enjoys doing the same for her readers. Through the gift of storytelling, she is able to bring little- and well-known people and events in African American history to life for young readers. She hopes that her stories will augment the classroom experience and inspire readers. J. P. lives in metro Atlanta and is the author of the *Careers in the US Military* and *Black Stories Matter* series.

ABOUT THE ILLUSTRATOR

Amanda Quartey Amanda lives in the UK and was born and bred in London. She has always loved to draw and has been doing so ever since she can remember. At the age of 14 she moved to Ghana and studied art in school. She later returned to the UK to study graphic design. Her artistic path deviated slightly when she studied Classics at college. Over the years, in a bid to return to her artistic roots, Amanda has built a professional illustration portfolio and is now loving every bit of her illustration career.

www.rourkeeducationalmedia.com

Quote source: Heise, Kenan. "Jackie Ormes, 68; Drew Comic Strip 'Torchy.'" *Chicago Tribune*, January 3, 1986.

Edited by: Tracie Santos
Illustrations by: Amanda Quartey
Cover and interior layout by: J.J. Giddings

Library of Congress PCN Data

Jackie Ormes / J. P. Miller
(Leaders Like Us)
ISBN 978-1-73164-930-0 (hard cover)
ISBN 978-1-73164-878-5 (soft cover)
ISBN 978-1-73164-982-9 (e-Book)
ISBN 978-1-73165-034-4 (ePub)
Library of Congress Control Number: 2021935551

Rourke Educational Media
Printed in the United States of America
01-1872111937